That's Betty!

The Story of
BETTY WHITE

For my mom, who taught me not just how to read, but its importance —G. B.
For funny, white-haired animal lovers everywhere, especially my mom — J. P.

Henry Holt and Company, *Publishers since 1866* • Henry Holt® is a registered trademark of Macmillan Publishing Group, LLC 120 Broadway, New York, NY 10271 • mackids.com • Text copyright © 2021 by Gregory Bonsignore. • Illustrations copyright © 2021 by Jennifer M. Potter. All rights reserved. • Our books may be purchased in bulk for promotional, educational, or business use. Please contact your local bookseller or the Macmillan Corporate and Premium Sales Department at (800) 221-7945 ext. 5442 or by email at MacmillanSpecialMarkets@macmillan.com. • Library of Congress Control Number: 2021906543 First edition, 2021 • Book design by Sharismar Rodriguez • Printed in China by RR Donnelley Asia Printing Solutions Ltd., Dongguan City, Guangdong Province • The art in this book was executed in Acryla gouache and digital media.
ISBN 978-1-250-79660-8

10 9 8 7 6 5 4 3 2 1

Gregory Bonsignore

Illustrated by **Jennifer M. Potter**

A WHO DID IT FIRST? BOOK
Henry Holt and Company
New York

Our teacher asked us each to pick a trailblazing woman for a presentation. And I thought . . .

Betty White couldn't be more trailblazing! She's an actress who starred in some of the very first TV shows and who has had the longest career in the history of television!

But my teacher wasn't so sure about the idea.

Hmm. Wouldn't you rather choose someone more . . . *traditional?*

And my classmates didn't even know who she was.

Betty who?

What did he say?

Betty *Friedan?*

Betty White! The most amazing entertainer ever!

I told my dads about my idea, and one of them wasn't so sure about it either.

I knew that if I was going to do this project on Betty, it had to be the best presentation EVER. Thankfully, my second-favorite person in the world, Darian the Vegetarian Librarian, was there to help.

"What's our adventure today?" he asked.

"Give me everything you have on 'White' comma 'Betty,' please!"

Just as I began assembling the world's greatest presentation on the world's greatest person, I heard a voice in the stacks.

"Hey, kid," some lady whispered. "Heard you're doing a presentation on Betty White, and I just happen to be an authority on that broad."

Before I could say anything, she continued, "She was born in Oak Park, Illinois, on January 17, 1922, to Christine and Horace."

I looked in my notes, and she was right!

"Betty got her start in radio," I continued.

"Her first big break on television was co-hosting *Hollywood on Television* with Al Jarvis, way back in 1949, when TV was brand-new!"

"You do know your stuff!" the lady said. "But did you also know that the show was *live*, for five and a half hours a day, six days a week?"

I didn't, so I added it to my notebook.

"Soon after that, she got her *own* show," the lady said.

"The Betty White Show." I smiled. "The show started in 1954. Betty hosted the show at a time when almost no other women worked in TV."

"Very true," she said. "Did you know that Betty also *produced* the show?"

"What does that mean?" I asked.

"The producer is the boss of the whole show," she explained, "and decides everything about how a program gets made."

"A producer oversees important stuff, like the advertisers,

the segments and songs,
and the casting.

"One of the people Betty cast was a dancer she loved named
Arthur Duncan. But some people didn't want her show
to feature a Black performer."

Maybe you could cast
someone more ...
traditional.

Live
with it!

"What did Betty do?"
I asked, scribbling
in my notebook.
    "She said,
'Live with it!'"

"Arthur's extraordinary talent was given center stage, dazzling the audience."

"And she gave Arthur TWICE as much screen time as before."
"That's Betty!" I cheered.

This lady obviously knew a whole lot about Betty White—more than I was finding in my books, even. "What happened next?" I asked.

The lady thought for a moment. "Well, Betty went on to be a guest on a number of game shows."

"She even found the great love of her life, Allen Ludden, on the set of the game show *Password* in 1961. Allen was the host, and Betty thought he was the most wonderful man she'd ever met."

"But this book says he was her *third* husband," I noted.

"Well, third time's the charm, kid!" the lady said.

"Betty hosted the Macy's Thanksgiving Day Parade for ten years and the Tournament of Roses Parade for twenty," I told the lady. "And she also starred in my two favorite shows of all time!"

MAMA'S FAMILY

"Betty starred in more than one hundred
TV shows and movies," she said.
"So, which ones are we
talking about, kid?"

YOU
ALWAYS
GET MORE
AT
THE WORLD'S
LARGEST STORE
Macy's

Life With Elizabeth

"The first of my favorites," I said, "was a very influential TV series from the 1970s called *The Mary Tyler Moore Show*—a feminist sitcom that showed women could do anything a man could do."

ON AIR

"And my other favorite show is *The Golden Girls*, which started in 1985. It's my dads' favorite show of all time."

The lady nodded. "That tracks."

"The show ran for seven seasons and showed that older people have full, meaningful, hilarious lives. Betty won *another* Emmy Award, this time for her portrayal of Rose Nylund."

Sandy Duncan, Rose . . . BETTY WHITE, you numbskull!

"Betty wasn't done yet. In 2010, when she was eighty-eight years old, she starred in a new show called *Hot in Cleveland*."

"That's right!" the lady said. "Betty set a Guinness World Record with that role, for the longest television career in history!"

"Say, kid. Do any of those books mention all the work Betty has done for her fantastic furry friends? Betty has always supported animal causes."

"Despite all of her achievements as an actress, Betty has said that she is, first and foremost, someone who loves animals."

"It says here that Betty was on the board of the American Humane Society," I added. "And that she has given hundreds of thousands of dollars to benefit animals!"

"Was it that much?" The lady gasped. "That's Betty, all right."

Just then, my dads came by to see if I was ready to go. I realized I had more than enough material to make the best presentation ever.

"Thanks for all your help," I said to the lady.

"My pleasure. You ring me if you need anything else."

But that night, I got nervous about my presentation the next day.

You know, kiddo, it's not too late to do a report on someone more traditional.

OR you could just do the one you love about Betty.

So I decided to call the lady from the library.

She picked up. "Hello, this is—"

"Hi, it's me. From the library. The one doing a landmark project on Betty White. I'm a little worried that . . ."

"That your presentation is going to be a little *too* different?" she asked warmly.

"Well . . . yeah," I said.

"Ya know, kid . . . I realized a long time ago, I couldn't look around at other people to figure out what was possible, what I should do with *my* life. I was an untraditional gal with untraditional dreams—

I just had to believe in myself and make it happen! Why, it wasn't until I wrote and starred in a school play that I realized what I wanted to do."

"That's funny," I said. "The same was true for Betty White."

"Is that so?" she said with a laugh. "Well, I'm sure that if Betty were here, she would tell you to hold tight to your dreams, and make tomorrow whatever the heck you want it to be, kid!"

The next day, my presentation was a big hit, maybe the best presentation ever.

Wow!

I was just about to take my seat when someone at the door called out, *"Bravo!"*

She did all that?!

She's amazing!

It was the lady from the library!
She looked so proud of me as she
grabbed a piece of cheesecake
and danced out of the class.

"Who was that?" my teacher asked.

And I realized . . .

TIMELINE

1922 – Betty Marion White is BORN!
Note! She was born in Oak Park, Illinois, on January 17.

1924 – Betty's family moves to California.

1939 – Betty graduates from Beverly Hills High School.

1941 – Betty volunteers during World War II driving military supplies.

Public domain via Wikimedia Commons

1953 – Betty premieres her first TV sitcom, *Life with Elizabeth*, which she stars in and produces.

1960 – Betty receives her star on the Hollywood Walk of Fame at 6747 Hollywood Boulevard.

1961 – Betty meets Allen Ludden.
Note! Though he proposed a number of times, she wouldn't say yes to marrying him till 1963!

1973 – Betty's character Sue Ann Nivens joins the cast of *The Mary Tyler Moore Show*.
Note! When they wrote the part, they wanted "an actress like Betty White," and never guessed they would get her!

1983 – Betty wins an Emmy for Outstanding Game Show Host for *Just Men*!
Note! She was the first woman to ever win an Emmy in that category.

1985 – Betty plays Rose Nylund on *The Golden Girls*, which premieres that year on NBC.

1987 – Betty wins the Humane Award from the American Veterinary Medical Association for her dedication to animals.

2010 – Betty becomes the oldest person to ever host *Saturday Night Live*.
Note! She won ANOTHER Emmy for this show, her fifth!

Associated Press

Back in St. Olaf...

2011 – Betty wins a Grammy for the audio recording of her bestselling memoir *If You Ask Me (And of Course You Won't)*.

2012 – Betty visits with President Barack Obama in the White House's Oval Office. *Note!* President Obama also recorded a happy birthday message for Betty's 90th birthday party special.

2015 – Betty finishes her last episode on *Hot in Cleveland*. *Note!* There are 128 episodes of the show.

2019 – Betty stars in *Toy Story 4* as Bitey White, a teething toy tiger.

2022 – Betty turns 100 years old!

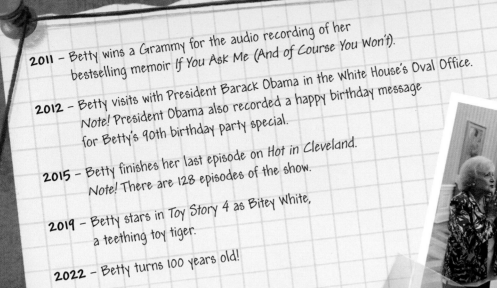

Pete Souza/the White House

SELECTED SOURCES

Boettcher, Steven J., dir. *Betty White, First Lady of Television*. 2018. Netflix.

Colucci, Jim. *Golden Girls Forever: An Unauthorized Look Behind the Lanai*. New York: Harper Design, 2016.

Fantozzi, Tony. "The Interviews: Betty White." Television Academy Foundation. June 4, 1997, video, 2:26:06, https://interviews.televisionacademy.com/interviews/betty-white#about.

Imdb.com (Resource used for various dates and casts: Accessed 2020).

Junger Witt, Paul, S. Harris, and T. Thomas, executive producers. *The Golden Girls*, Buena Vista Television, 1985–92.

Paley Center for Media (Assorted interviews and archived materials: Accessed 2020).

Pioneers of Television: Sitcoms. TV Programs on Iowa Public Television. Iptv.org, 2015.

White, Betty. *Here We Go Again: My Life in Television*. New York: Scribner, 1995.

White, Betty. *If You Ask Me (And of Course You Won't)*. New York: G.P. Putnam's Sons, 2011.